Camping With
Mr. McDoogle

Written and Illustrated By:

Marie Whitton

For My Husband
Greg

For My Children
Gregory, Ann-Marie &
Kimberly

For My
Grandchildren

What does Mr. McDoogle's
campgrounds have in store,
Will it be a bore?
Come on in and let's see,
There is a small campsite fee.

Here is a perfect site to set up camp,
Take out the tent, sleeping bags, food and
even the lamp.
Stack up the wood,
Getting ready for a campfire - it will be
good.

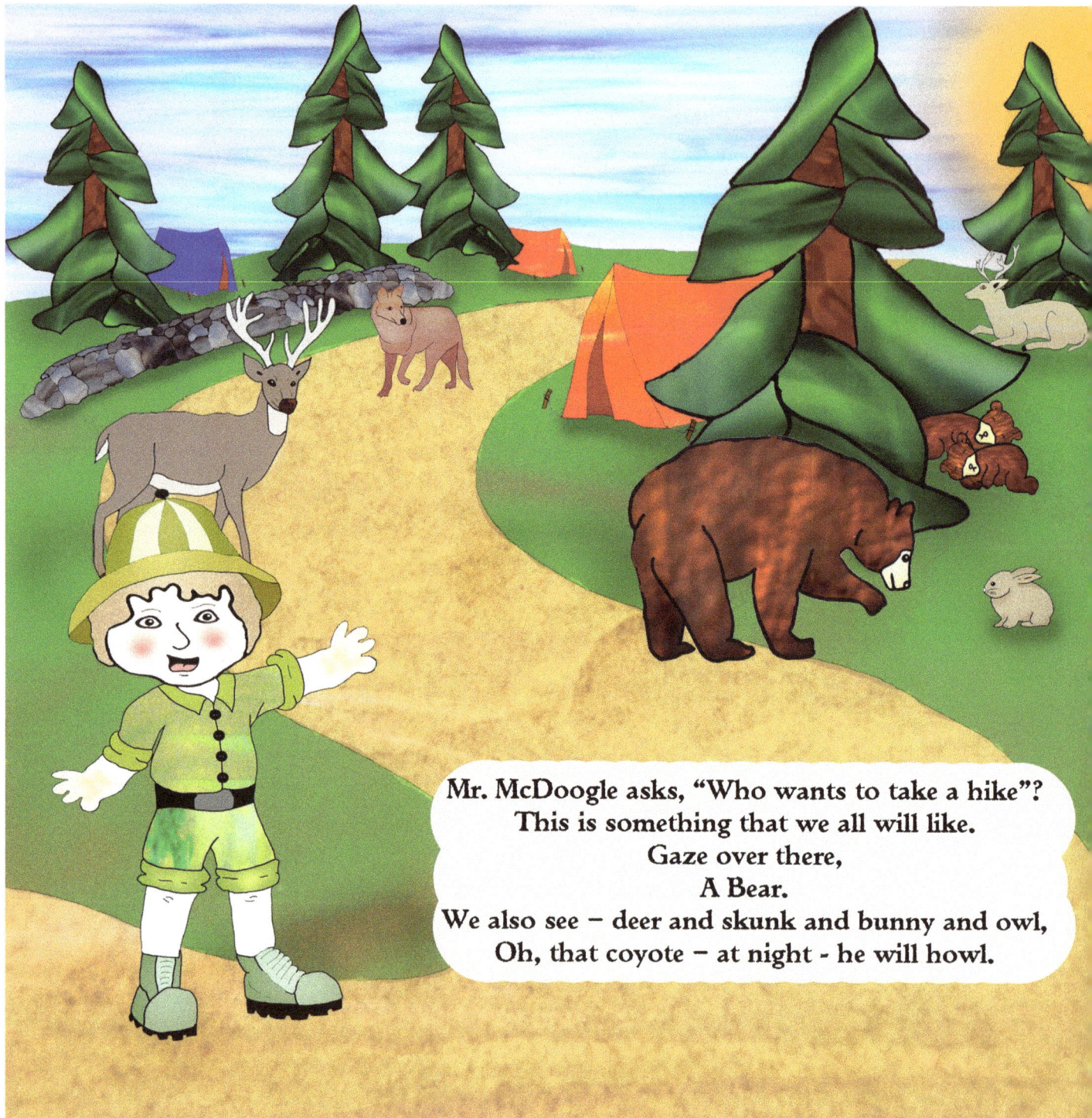

Mr. McDoogle asks, "Who wants to take a hike"?
This is something that we all will like.
Gaze over there,
A Bear.
We also see − deer and skunk and bunny and owl,
Oh, that coyote − at night - he will howl.

Time for lunch,
We just won't munch.
There is nothing like cooking hot dogs on a fire,
Of this - we will not tire.

After lunch, it is time to rest,
By playing cards - with family - it is the best.

We can hear the fire crackling,
And the children are not cackling.
Instead they are marshmallow roasting,
A S'Mores party they are hosting.

The stars are so clear and bright,
Just twinkling in the night, it was a
beautiful sight.
Under the stars the children will sleep,
All night - we did not hear a peep.

Time to go Fishing - to the kids
Mr. McDoogle did say,
It was such a perfect day.
Fishing they had the knack,
To the campsite - they went back.
The bucket was full of Fish,
So - we will cook our favorite dish.

Having lots of fun,
In the Lake - in the sun.
Going canoeing was our first,
With excitement we did burst.

Around the corner we smelled a familiar smell,
A smell that we knew so very well.
Mom and Dad are cooking,
In the pot we are looking.
We are so hungry we can't wait to eat.
Let's set the table and take our seat.

The lake was cold and deep,
We decided to swim and take a
leap.
Enjoying the warmth of the
sun,
Swimming it was cool and fun.

The fire was a blaze,
The flames were putting us in a daze.
Decided to play a tune,
Under the shine of the moon.

Found out what Mr. McDoogle's
campgrounds had in store,
It was not a bore?
Lots to see and do – our memories are dear,
Can't wait to come back next year.

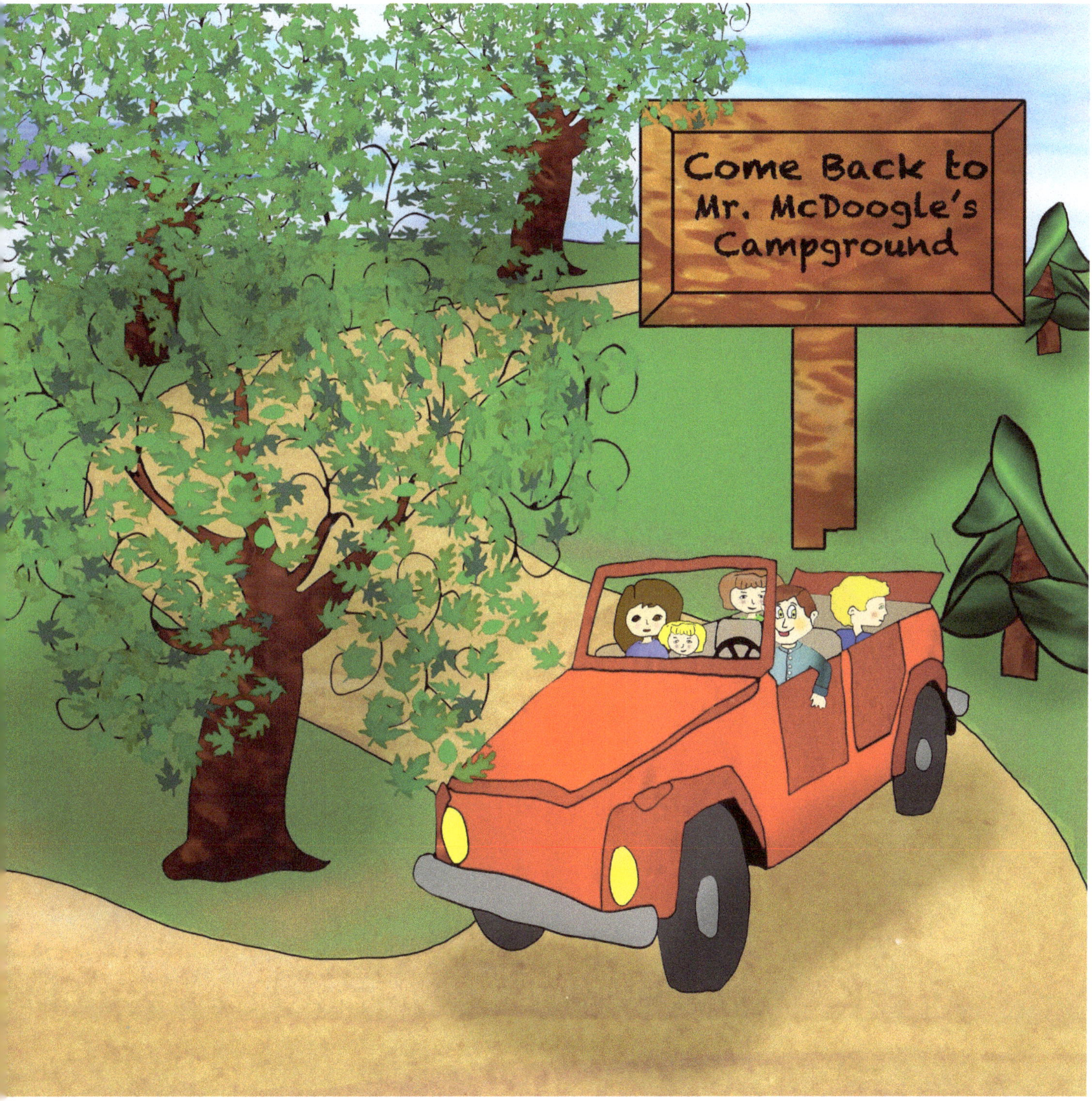
Come Back to
Mr. McDoogle's
Campground